FACET BOOKS

SOCIAL ETHICS SERIES

FACET fb BOOKS

SOCIAL ETHICS SERIES — 4

Franklin Sherman, General Editor

Christianity in a Divided Europe

by HANNS LILJE

FORTRESS PRESS   PHILADELPHIA

The Burge Memorial Lecture delivered at Church House, Westminster, London, on March 8, 1961. Reprinted by permission.

Published by Fortress Press, 1965

Introduction © 1965 by Fortress Press

Library of Congress Catalog Card Number 65-12764

8409A65   Printed in U. S. A.   UB3018

Introduction

THE wall across Berlin. Has there ever been a barrier which so wholly combined the functions of being an actual instrument of division, and the most vivid possible symbol of it?

Bishop Lilje's prophetic lecture, which was delivered just before the erection of the wall, helps us to understand the background of that event. He traces the present division of Europe into "Eastern" and "Western" spheres back to certain fateful decisions made during the closing months of World War II. These decisions determined where the dividing line should be drawn. But the actual content that subsequently filled the two spheres thus marked off was determined by the ideological and political situation; above all, by the inrush of an expansive communism from the east.

The challenge of communism to the Christian churches has seldom been dealt with so incisively as in this essay. Not self-defense but self-examination is the prevailing mood of the discussion. How can the churches match in their own life and thought the vigor of this movement, which so appeals to the secular mentality of our time? Bishop Lilje, while fully aware of the sinister aspects of communism (see, for example, what he says about the "double language" required under communist regimes) is equally aware that its challenge cannot be met by denunciation, but only by the provision of a more attractive alternative. This latter cannot consist merely in the repetition of familiar Christian slogans or in the effort to restore some vanished form of "Christian social order." For in the West of Europe as well as in the East, the "Christian epoch" is at an end; the whole era of the unquestioned predominance of Christianity in European civilization that began with the conversion of the Roman Empire, is now over. Only an honest recognition of this fact and a reconsideration of their own life and work in light of it, says Bishop Lilje, will enable the churches to preserve — for the benefit of humanity as a whole — what was precious in that epoch.

The author's own life experience has prepared him well to understand what is at stake in the encounter between Christianity and alien ideologies. Born in Hannover, Germany, in 1899, he studied theology and art history at Göttingen, Leipzig, and Zurich. From the mid-1920's onward he served as a leader of the student Christian movement in Germany and as a German representative at many ecumenical assemblies. It was his contacts with foreign churches that led to his arrest and imprisonment by the Gestapo in 1944. His memorable book *The Valley of the Shadow* (Philadelphia: Muhlenberg Press, 1950) describes his experiences at that time.

From 1935 to 1947, Hanns Lilje served as general secretary of the Lutheran World Convention, and from 1952 to 1957 as president of the Lutheran World Federation. He has been equally active in the World Council of Churches and its predecessor movements, and serves as a member of both the central committee and the executive committee of the council. Elected bishop of the Church of Hannover in 1947, he has been since 1955 the presiding bishop of the United Evangelical Lutheran Church of Germany. He is also vice-chairman of the Evangelical Church in Germany (EKiD), and a president of the European Council of Churches.

Bishop Lilje's concern for social and cultural questions has been expressed in his editorship of the weekly newspaper *Sonntagsblatt,* published in Hamburg, as well as in his leadership in the founding of the evangelical academies just after World War II. He is well known as a preacher and lecturer in both Great Britain and the United States. Several of his books have been published in English translation, among them his valuable study of the present-day significance of Martin Luther entitled *Luther Now* (Philadelphia: Muhlenberg Press, 1952). Others are listed under "For Further Reading."

Most of the Latin phrases used in the essay are explained in the text itself: *reservatio mentalis* — a mental reservation; *atheismus militans, atheismus subtilis sive philosophicus, atheismus practicus* — the three types of atheism distinguished by the author (militant atheism, "subtle" or philosophical atheism, practical atheism); *securitas* and *certitudo* — "security" and "certainty," the former a kind of personal safety and self-assurance which the Christian (according to Luther — and Lilje) cannot expect to have, the latter the Christian's characteristic firm conviction and courageous trust in God.

The English text of the essay was prepared by Bishop Lilje himself and was first published by SCM Press, London. For the present American edition, a few stylistic changes have been made, and the footnotes have been altered so as to refer, when possible, to American editions of the works cited.

FRANKLIN SHERMAN

Mansfield College
Oxford, England
September, 1964

Contents

1

THE DIVISION OF EUROPE
AS A FACT OF OUR TIME

TWO outstanding facts are likely to dominate the development of politics during the rest of our century.

The first has to do with *the end of colonialism.* The rule of the white man has come to its close; new nations are being shaped and enter the scene of world history. Nobody can foresee the outcome of this epochal change. We are living through an upheaval of gigantic dimensions.

The other fact is that alarming growth of the world's population which goes by the significant name of *the population explosion.* Gloomy perspectives present themselves to the human mind. While it took the human race several centuries to increase twofold the speed has changed tremendously recently. By the end of this century the world's population will have doubled twice. Every other human being is going to be a Chinese by that time, and as to living space for the individual, statistics reveal a more pessimistic outlook.

Christianity has tried to face these problems. The World Council of Churches through its various agencies has done remarkable work in analyzing these phenomena and suggesting ways and means of meeting the challenge involved.[1]

But there is still that third element of the political situation which has been the undercurrent of world politics since the end of World War II — *the division of Europe.* The fact that the world was split up into two ideological power blocks has had a more lasting effect upon the whole development than any other comparable event. For here we do not encounter one of the merely biological factors of history or one of the usual political arrangements by which the end of World War II was marked. The characteristic feature of the East-West conflict is the combination of power politics and ideological struggle. This makes it necessary that Christianity should face this problem in two respects: (*a*) on a political basis, as far as the preservation of world peace is concerned, and (*b*) from the point of view of philosophical and religious conviction, if it comes to the specific ideological outlook. One may safely say that this conflict of ideas is the outstanding challenge of our generation, and that is the reason why Christians have to rethink this problem over and over again.

They must do so, however, observing two or three important presuppositions.

In the first place objectivity is required, and a great deal of it indeed. In the present political struggle the outlook is so frequently blurred by prejudices of all

[1] See, for example, the excellent paper by Prof. E. de Vries on "Population Growth and Christian Responsibility," published in *The Ecumenical Review,* XVIII, I (October, 1960), 36 ff.

kinds that one of the main contributions of Christians must be an attempt to evaluate conditions in an unprejudiced manner. Unbiased precision of thought should be one of the noblest forms of Christian behavior in the sphere of politics. In it the Christian will always stand for truth and justice, and he will always maintain that there can be no lasting solution if either one is being disregarded. But he will present the case of truth and justice in a sober and balanced way, giving credit to the other's point of view as much as to his own. He will carefully avoid sharpening the issue and embittering his opponent.

Man's natural inclination will lead him to the idea of "friend-foe-relationship," to borrow the main concept of Prof. Carl Schmitt's political philosophy.[2] While this category may be an accurate description of the reality of political life it turns into a most dangerous idea if it is made the norm or standard of political behavior. Lenin's political philosophy did not shrink from drawing this conclusion and considered "implacability" an essential element of political struggle.[3] Racial and political prejudice, hatred and the desire for extirpation of the opponent — these are the logical consequences of this attitude.

The Christian opposition to this is not primarily centered around love, but based on objectivity. A fair and just judgment will accept what is good in the enemy's general attitude and will not overdo one's own point of

[2] Carl Schmitt, *Der Begriff des Politischen,* 1932.
[3] Cf. Lenin, *State and Revolution,* (New York: International Publishers, ch. I, section 1, "The State as the Product of the Irreconcilability of Class Antagonisms."

view. All propagandistic exaggerations prove to be dangerous to any reasonable and lasting settlement of political controversies.

But in order to achieve this objectivity, another presupposition must be stated. Since history has given ample proof that man usually does not follow the suggestions of reason, objectivity must be based on a deeper and more solid foundation. It is to be found in the Christian faith. It is a certain spiritual courage which is required and, at the same time, the spirit of reconciliation in a very practical and realistic form.

Courage is required because any attempt to attain objectivity will meet with certain disapproval from the so-called political "realist." To this type of politician, a kind not infrequently encountered, the Christian call for objectivity will be troublesome and disquieting. Every consideration of conscience will disturb the complacency and self-assurance of mere expediency. And Christian thinking will be even more definitely opposed to the widespread tendency of political fanaticism.

The spirit of reconciliation is a basic requirement if a lasting solution of a serious political crisis is sought. A merely formalistic understanding of "justice" will never be sufficient in such a case. A real liquidation of hostilities cannot be reached except by the firm decision to bury the past and to look into the future. This can best be done by the simple human application of the spirit of reconciliation. Mutual forgiveness can be a very realistic element of politics. In this specific sense, the majority of the problems which we sum up under the term of "cold war" constitute a tremendous chal-

lenge to the Christian church of today. Pride and prejudice breed fear, at least in the sphere of politics, and
fear is the worst possible counselor.

This, then, in very broad outlines, is the background
over against which we have to consider our specific
problem of the division of Europe.

ORIGINS OF THE DIVISION

THERE is little doubt that the division of Europe is one of the most fateful facts, if not the most tragic fact, of postwar European history. Among the many strange and unnatural dividing lines which political developments after World War II created, that line which divides Germany into two parts seems to be one of the most neuralgic ones, because it was bound to create a state of continuous unrest. For this new frontier is unreasonable, not only because it divides Germans from Germans, but also because the whole world has to carry the burden which lies primarily on German shoulders. A problem which seemed to be confined to German history has developed into a prominent problem of world politics today. It is safe to state that there will be no world peace unless a settlement of this problem is reached.

All this has been said over and over again, and repetition does not help very much. The question which we have to face, however, is whether there is a more helpful interpretation of this fateful fact and what the possibilities for Christians and the Christian churches are in a situation like this.

This calls for a twofold task, a careful analysis of the situation and a consideration of possible solutions. The second task cannot be fulfilled without careful thought about the spiritual possibilities as well as the political ones.

A short historical survey of the development will prove to be useful.

If we try to fix a date, we must go back to the Yalta conference of 1945.[4] The three leading statesmen of the Allies, President Franklin D. Roosevelt of the United States, Sir Winston Churchill of Great Britain, and Marshal Joseph Stalin of the Soviet Union, decided at that time that Germany should be divided up in order to avoid any resurgence of its military power. Modern historical research has proved in the meantime that British observers realized the full impact of these decisions and tried to change it, while President Roosevelt apparently had even less knowledge of the geographical details of Europe than President Wilson after World War I. There seems to be general agreement that he overestimated the friendliness and flexibility of Joseph Stalin. Sir Winston Churchill and Field-Marshal Montgomery have given proof that they estimated affairs more realistically. Montgomery wanted to carry on the war with such vigor and energy that the western Allies would occupy Berlin, Prague, and Warsaw in

[4] In addition to the numerous memoirs by Sir Winston Churchill, Field-Marshal Montgomery, and others, cf. especially Alan Bullock, *Hitler, A Study in Tyranny* (New York: Harper, 1952; rev. ed., 1960).

order to keep the Russians at that line. Churchill seems to have suggested a similar proposal at the Yalta conference.[5] But at that time their influence was too limited. So the decision was made which drew the line in the heart of Germany. The conference at Potsdam in April, 1945, added to these miscalculations by yielding to the Russians a new frontier which followed the Elbe and Werra rivers, thereby handing to the Russians a large part of the territory between the present zonal border line and Berlin.

Today we realize that this was a mistake of historical importance.

While at the Yalta conference the Allies, in the words of Alan Bullock, "patched up their differences and contrived an agreement which, however, impermanent, outlasted Hitler,"[6] the situation became immediately worse when, following up the Potsdam agreement, the American troops withdrew from the line first agreed upon and handed over the provinces of Saxony and Thuringia to the Russians, thus enlarging the sphere of occupation for the benefit of Russia. In this way the whole problem of Berlin was artificially created since the western Allies gave up not only two important German provinces but also their control of the way to Berlin. The present difficulty of Berlin could have been avoided if the western Allies had stood by their previous decision.

---

[5] *Memoirs of Field-Marshal Montgomery* (Cleveland: World Publishing Co., 1958), pp. 330-333, esp. p. 332: "The Americans could not understand that it was of little avail to win the war strategically if we lost it politically."

[6] Bullock, *op. cit.*, p. 712.

A deeper insight into history may come to the conclusion that it is only one of the cruel consequences of history that today that country out of which the catastrophe of World War II arose has to pay the price, by having this dividing line of European and world politics in the heart of its own territory. But that does not do away with the fact that today world politics as a whole has to deal with the consequences of this most unfortunate decision.

Let me explain this. The division of Germany is not an isolated problem. It involves the division of Europe as a whole. The Scandinavian countries remained neutral as they had before; but the rest of Eastern Europe came under Russian domination. The Communist sphere of influence in Eastern Europe was solidified by treaties and other subsequent events. Today this line of division is firmly established from the frontier of Mecklenburg, which is to say, a few miles east of Hamburg, to Helmstedt, which is a few miles east of Brunswick, and down to the Bavarian border.

A few additional observations may be of interest. This dividing line constitutes a frontier which is more strongly fortified than any other frontier in Europe. For this line is guarded by trenches and barbed wire. A no man's land has been put in between the immediate frontier line and the country beyond. Sentries patrol the other side of the Iron Curtain. A passport control of the strictest type is carried out and vigorously applied in a surveillance which leaves no movement of the visitor from the West uncovered. Even if there were no different political and economic systems involved, this frontier line would have to be considered as unnatural, because it divides people who speak the same language, are of the same racial and ethnic origin, have derived their spiritual values from the same cultural and religious sources. The fact that two different political and economic systems have been developed since the end of World War II makes the situation even more difficult. While on the Eastern side of the Iron Curtain the people have lived now for nearly thirty years under a dictatorial type of government, the Western part has in the meantime regained political freedom and established a modern democracy. The whole way of life has developed in such a different direction, and the whole setup of political and social order has made such a deep impact upon the two parts of Germany, that a reunion which is fervently hoped for by every German can be considered only with gravest concern. On that day the gigantic task would have to be faced how the two parts of Germany, which have taken such different courses, can rediscover a common basis.

A really careful study of the historical presuppositions cannot confine itself to these historic dates only. We must try to understand the background of this development. The ideological conflict which splits Europe and the world today has exercised its influence on Europe since the great Russian revolution of 1917. But while the Germans understood to a certain extent that the necessities of war made it advisable for the Allies to join hands with the Russians even for a limited period, the depth of the real difference became apparent immediately after the end of the war, especially in the way in which the Russians dealt with the problems of justice during the Nuremberg trials. That the western Allies should have deemed it wise to join hands with the Russians certainly would never have happened if it had not been for the war which Hitler set loose. Without this there would never have been the necessity for the Yalta powers to form a military alliance, and one may well imagine that no division of Europe would ever have taken place. So it may seem not to be too farfetched to put the blame for the division of Europe today in the last analysis upon Nazism.[7]

A most important consequence of this development as we see it today is the breakup of the unity of Christian Europe. Now every student of history knows that this problem requires careful definition. Europe as a Christian unity may be drawing to its close anyhow. It seems to be a strange coincidence that there is not only

[7] I may be permitted to add, however, that the history of Germany's responsibility for the Third Reich is not as simple as that. A careful and objective description would have to include some of the blunders committed by Western powers before and immediately after Hitler came into power. If democratic Germany had been given more of a chance in the fateful years 1929-32 things would have taken a different course. And if the Western powers would have taken a firmer stand against Hitler, they might have helped Germany to a better and more effective resistance. And finally, if the British government would have listened to people like Bonhoeffer, who in the now famous Stockholm talks of 1942 persuaded the Bishop of Chichester, Dr. Bell, to approach the British government with a view to some sort of helpful declaration in favor of the opposition, at least the last and very bloody year of war might have been spared.

It is always a sad business to revise history which happened. No reflection on that time can change facts. But it seems wise not to suppress these considerations entirely.

[For an account of the talks to which Bishop Lilje refers see the reports and correspondence in Dietrich Bonhoeffer, *Gesammelte Schriften,* ed. Eberhard Bethge (Munich: Christian Kaiser Verlag, 1958), Vol. I, pp. 372-413. —Editor.]

the powerful progress of a political system which is avowedly based upon an atheistic philosophy, but that at the same time an alarming process of secularization is spreading through the Western countries of Europe which amounts in some places to complete paganization. It may well be that the Christian epoch of Europe is at stake anyhow — communism or no communism. But on the other hand it goes without saying that the political success of worldwide communism has speeded up this development and given the whole problem a terrific practical effect. There is no use shedding tears over the fact that a long and blessed epoch of history seems to come to its close. But it is even worse not to realize the impact of a crisis of history such as we witness today. This is no mere speculation of the church historian; rather, this change has to do with the foundation beliefs of our whole Western political philosophy. For there is no use in maintaining freedom and a responsible type of government unless the spiritual foundations upon which all these magnificent concepts should be based are clearly kept in mind.

It would, however, be premature to abandon the Christian epoch of European history. The historical significance of Europe is not only a phenomenon of the past. That long period in which the smallest of the continents took the lead has to face the most difficult test in all its history. So far there is no reason to consider this chapter of history to be closed. On the one hand, all spiritual heresies of our age are derived from European sources. There is literally not a single one of the influential political philosophies of our day that has not sprung from Europe. On the other hand, Europe still has the capacity of radical new thought. It is true that some of the most radical types of philosophy of our day again have their origin in European thinking. And at any rate the liquidation of Europe's Christian past would not be an affair of a few years. We must realize that all of us are engaged in a spiritual war of great dimensions. Our task, therefore, is to consider the philosophical background of the present division of Europe.

3

PHILOSOPHICAL BACKGROUND
OF THE DIVISION

LET me make a few preliminary remarks.

There is no need to explain the difference of political ideologies. The clash of Marxist ideology with Western political philosophy is well known and does not require further description. I should like to draw attention to one point only. The dictatorial system claims total allegiance from its citizens: that is to say, an allegiance which consists not only in formalistic obedience. But the claim is that obedience should be based upon conviction. Now it goes without saying that this conviction cannot be taken for granted on the part of all citizens. This leads to a remarkable phenomenon which one must recognize. That part of the population which does not agree with the fundamental doctrines of the governing group learns to speak a double-tongued language. There is a distinction between what they say and between what they really believe. This, of course, leads to a state of mind which is not at all wholesome. In every dictatorial system we find this curiously curved, depraved type of language where for all appearances agreement with official doctrine is established and where at the same time a completely different mental attitude is maintained, a *reservatio mentalis* on a large scale. This may be possible for a short while, and may be excused as a sort of ruse without which existence would not be possible. But the difficulties grow from year to year. That part of the population which feels the burden more than any other is the younger generation. From the very beginning they have to face the tremendous difficulty of adjusting their speech and behavior to official requirements which they do not share by conviction. Naturally there are three different reactions. There are those who are able and have enough intellectual strength to live under the pressure of this double-talk and the mental strain it involves. There are others who do not. They may submit out of sheer resignation; they give up and adapt themselves. But in doing so they lose their integrity and their moral self-esteem. There are others who are fascinated by official doctrine and accept it wholeheartedly. They, of course, meet with the outspoken disapproval of the other group. So there are, on the one hand, those who in a very servile way try to do justice to the government's requests, and on the other hand the silent group of grumbling opponents who try to maintain their spiritual and intellectual integrity.

One of the worst aspects of this situation is the distorted concept of truth and falsehood. On the basis of Marxist dialectics, telling a lie is something entirely different from what the bourgeois thinks. Those who have accepted Marxism can no longer be challenged by those standards of truth which Western tradition has accepted for centuries as the basis of every human conversation. A fact may be told in a very different way according to the usefulness which the speaker attaches to it. Propaganda is just a milder form of brainwashing. But it may reach such proportions as to destroy entirely the common concept of truth. That is the main reason why arguing does not lead very far in discussions with Marxists.

Let us not forget, however, that two other aspects of Marxism must be added. The one is the conviction that power can and must be used in order to enforce the Marxist truth. At the same time the fundamental concepts of Marxism are no mere theories: the scientific basis of Marxist thinking makes it necessary to put all these convictions into practice. The person who will not adapt himself to the Marxist pattern of thought will be excluded from the advantages of education and similar prospects in life. At a very early stage — much earlier than the average young person in the Western world may think — those who live under that dictatorial system have to make tremendous decisions which are meant to shape their entire future. So it may well be that a young person who does not fully embrace Marxist beliefs has only the choice between really accepting these (or at least feigning acceptance) or being excluded from the university and other places of higher education. It is not sufficient to consider this choice as a spiritual struggle only. The Marxist authorities never shrink from enforcing their truth by these very tangible means of pressure.

Still, all this is just the picture as it presents itself from the outside. Let us try to dig deeper into the underlying spiritual elements. We cannot here give a full evaluation of Marxist philosophy. Suffice it to say that we have to deal with a very precise type of philosophical thought which claims to be based on scientific thinking and exclusively so, and which at the same time constitutes a challenge. Here is a philosophy which requires practical obedience at every point.

The great thinkers of Marxism must be classified in a very different way. Lenin was a sort of genius, while Stalin seems to have been much more of a schoolmaster type of thinker. How far Nikita Khrushchev is to be rated among the intellectuals is a problem still to be solved. We have to reckon with a clear-cut, well-defined type of thought, and there is more than one point where friction seems unavoidable. That again makes it necessary to lay bare the elements of this spiritual struggle we have to face.

One more annotation on history. Our theme is, of course, not new. There is a wealth of literature on the philosophical importance of Marxism, and there is no shortage of contributions given from a Christian point of view. I may mention very briefly only two very important publications. Mr. Robert Tobias' *Communist-Christian Encounter in East Europe* gives a very careful and full-sized evaluation of the problem.[8] We should also draw attention to the writings of one of the greatest thinkers of our days, the Russian philosopher

---

[8] Robert Tobias, *Communist-Christian Encounter in East Europe* (Indianapolis: Butler University, 1956).

Nicolas Berdyaev (1874-1948).[9] He was well equipped to deal with these problems, because he was converted twice — namely from Christianity (or maybe from a nihilism which was only slightly tainted by Christian influences) to communism, and from communism to Christianity. When in 1922 he was forced to give up his professorial chair he moved to Western Europe, first to Germany and later to France. One great blessing followed. By the very fact that he had to face the Western world, he became one of the great bridge builders between Eastern and Western thought. He interpreted the depth and richness of Russian spiritual tradition to the West and at the same time he was forced to express himself in the rational and more precise terms of Western philosophical tradition. His book on truth and falsehood in communism must be considered one of the classics in the philosophical exchange between East and West.

But the philosophical background of Marxism must also be seen in a wider context.

Our age could be called an atheistic one. We are referring not only to the specific "free thinker" type of nonreligious person. We have in mind the whole mental atmosphere of our generation. Atheism in this sense means a type of thinking which does not take into account any concept of God. Nobody can overlook the tremendous change in the mental attitude of our generation which is influenced to such an extent by scientific thought that other forms of philosophizing

[9] Most of Berdyaev's numerous writings have been translated into English.

seem to be outdated. This is true of our religious and Christian heritage also. In this sense, Marxism in its religious aspects is not an isolated phenomenon. There are many parallels in Western thought. This seems to be one of the immediate results of the spiritual struggle pervading Europe, that we cannot be satisfied by denouncing Marxist atheism or atheistic Marxism, but that we have to accept the manifold challenge which it includes.

This has to do, in the first place, with political and economic questions. A powerful political system has arisen in the East, and Western politics have to decide how they are going to meet this challenge. Combined with it is the claim to a new economic order of human society, and again the West has to make up its mind how to meet this challenge also. But the deeper we go, the more clearly we realize that our task cannot be fulfilled by considering the political and economic aspects only. We have to live up to the challenge in the spiritual field. If we want to do this not merely by repeating ironclad formulas, but by doing some real thinking, we cannot overlook the fact that philosophy and religion play an important role in meeting the challenge.

It will be wise therefore to consider the three different types of atheism which we find in our age. There is *atheismus militans,* militant atheism as presented by Eastern Marxism; there is *atheismus subtilis sive philosophicus,* the subtle type of Western philosophical atheism; and finally *atheismus practicus,* practical atheism. While the Eastern variation of atheism is apparently more precise, more scientific, and certainly more rationalistic, Western atheistic philosophy seems to have unfathomable depths which we shall have to explore.

An interesting illustration of Eastern atheism is a small pamphlet issued a few years ago by a professor of philosophy of Moscow University. The title is *Religious Superstition and the Damage It Does.*[10] A clear and precise title! There can be no doubt what the author has in mind. Religion is denounced as sheer superstition; the author does not shrink from describing, in no uncertain terms, what damage is being caused by this attitude. The Western reader is at first sight appalled by the apparent simplicity if not naïveté of this professor's style of thinking. But on second thought, we discover several aspects which we have to consider rather carefully.

Let me point out three characteristic features.

In the first place, there seems to prevail a simplicity of language and thought which is in sharp contrast to certain types of Western philosophy in which a complicated style seems to be the only sure indication of depth of thought. In this Russian thinker we meet the opposite. This simplicity does not leave any doubt or ambiguity. The simple structure of each sentence conveys the impression of utmost clarity. There is no room for doubt.

Now this, of course, calls for further consideration. Here are two conflicting aspects. On the one hand this

---

[10] I have only the German edition at my disposal: *Der religiöse Aberglaube und seine Schädlichkeit.*

type of thinking shrinks from all skepticism and avoids criticism. But on the other hand it has the advantage of being simple, clear, and useful.

The absence of any skeptical element in the official expositions of Marxist philosophy is dangerous to independent thought. It is one of the deep insights of Western philosophy, which never can be given up again, that only that type of thought is of any philosophic and scientific value which can face skepticism and stand the test of criticism. No dictatorial system can permit any free and independent thought in this sense. Its basis is and always will be the most standardized and static type of "truth." There are more hard-and-fast dogmas in Marxism than in any comparable period of church history. But still this simplicity seems to be the guarantee of security. The philosopher of a totalitarian ideology is sure of himself and his doctrine. And so he cannot permit any uncertainty or critical examination of the foundation beliefs of official Marxist thought. Again there is no doubt that this useful element makes it possible to train people's minds, and to shape them in any way which seems desirable to the officials of the regime.

This allergy to skepticism is natural to the genuine Marxist, because in his view there is no reason for any doubt. A deep and fervent optimism underlies Marxism — an understanding of man which is certain that man can be formed according to the communist program, and a concept of society which is absolutely sure of success. The eschatology of Marxism is colored with the flaming red of hope. It is sin to doubt or to hesitate. This victorious enthusiasm leaves no room for twisted language.

Another aspect is the claim to a strictly scientific basis of Marxism. Karl Marx himself started out with the conviction that the fate of human society could be shaped by applying the methods of modern economic sciences. It is true that he created a militant (and not entirely objective) sociology, and later propaganda has done much to obscure the purely scientific method. But up to this day the Marxist philosopher boasts that all his insights (including his insights into religion, if there is such a thing) are based on science in the strict sense of the word. It would not be difficult to point out the weakness of such a belief, and we would not have to take refuge in classical Christian thought in refuting this claim. Ludwig Marcuse, who in spite of an interesting visit to Moscow is far from being an adept of communism, and at the same time is anything but a Christian thinker, has in one of his recent books[11] a masterful exposition of why the superiority of scientific thinking in the Western academic tradition is a debatable phenomenon. It is *one* approach to reality among others; if we confine ourselves to it, we limit our access to reality. Overestimating science in the communist fashion is the sign of a youthful immaturity in the intellectual field. One of the main objections to this type of thought is that it will always be unable to face tragedy. And, alas, the world is full of tragedies. But these subtleties do not bother the Marxist thinker. He pushes

[11] Ludwig Marcuse, *Pessimismus* (Hamburg, 1953).

them aside as "alienations" which will be overcome in due time. And we have to accept his claim to "scientific" thinking as it stands.

This leads to the third element, which is of the most important practical significance. Marxist philosophy is the opposite of noncommittal thought which is so prevalent in the Western world. If these statements are true, then man has to draw certain consequences. He has to accept and to obey. In its way this third element is very impressive indeed. It explains the undeniable success of Marxism in the world of today, in which it has been able to subdue one-third of mankind.

4

THE CHALLENGE OF COMMUNISM

IT HAS rightly been said that if Christianity wants to meet the challenge of communism it must do so in an unprejudiced manner. It is characteristic of the Christian's attitude that in dealing with communism he does not follow the easy equation between Western democracy and the Christian way of life. He also cannot be satisfied by merely formalistic considerations. More than that is required.

But still it proves to be helpful, to suggest very briefly how Christianity and the traditional life of our theology and preaching does compare with the three characteristics of the atheistic propaganda of Marxism.

Its first element, its simplicity, constitutes a real and serious challenge to Christianity. It is not sufficient to point to the artificialities of our traditional theological language. There are certain subjects of theology which just cannot be explained simply. The depth and richness of the Christian faith cannot be watered down to shallow superficiality. But, on the other hand, there can be no doubt whatsoever that modern man's mind has either drifted away from traditional Christian speech or has been shaped very largely by modern scientific language. I share the opinion that while man's scientific thought has been developed during recent decades in a considerable way, his capacity for understanding religious and spiritual categories has not kept pace. This is the reason why clarity of language is required in presenting the gospel. There is no need to emphasize that this clarity does not consist in superficial abbreviations, but must be the final product of careful and solid thinking. To my mind William Temple, the late Archbishop of Canterbury, is one of the outstanding examples of that lucidity of mind which made simplicity of expression possible. It has been well said: if you cannot say simply what you believe, you either don't understand what you are talking about or you don't really believe what you say.

In order to save myself from any misunderstanding, let me add one more observation. Luther's classical distinction between *securitas* and *certitudo* is bound to affect our theological language too. There is a difference between shallow, superficial self-assurance (about which Bernanos has a few excellent remarks[12]) and that certainly of faith which is akin to the "persuasion" of which Paul speaks in the concluding words of the eighth chapter to the Romans. No theological or ecclesiastical jargon will have any lasting effect which shrinks from hard thinking and tries to avoid the tremendous intellectual efforts of modern theology. We

[12] Georges Bernanos, *The Diary of a Country Priest,* tr. Pamela Morris (New York: Image Books, 1954), p. 42: "The priest who descends from the pulpit of Truth, with a mouth like a hen's vent, a little hot but pleased with himself, he's not been preaching: at best he's been purring like a tabby-cat."

cannot go back behind the line drawn by Karl Barth, Rudolf Bultmann, and Paul Tillich. But let us not lose sight of the sense of victory which permeates Marxist thought. Let us try to meet the energy of the Marxists, their optimism, their hope, and let us not confine the Christian witness to a difficult, sinuous "eschatological" language, which reaches the esoteric expert only.

The second characteristic is even more serious. The claim of Marxist atheism to be based exclusively upon scientific thinking is superficial and naïve, but still it includes a very important aspect of modern life. Science, research, discovery, technical progress — all this means so much to modern man that no approach to reality will be taken seriously by him which cannot compare with this precision of thought. In this sense Marxist thinking is superior to any superficial religious emotionalism. Precision of language and thought seems indispensable in a generation which believes in the encyclopedia, in statistics, in experimentation, and other expressions of the scientific mind. Too frequently Christians who mean well have replaced clear belief by emotional generalities. There is also that dangerous type of syncretism which seems to be the latest fashion in Western mentality and which combines in a rather thoughtless way humanitarianisms of all sorts with certain remnants of Christian faith and social ethics. Christianity would be well advised, if it would take up this challenge and try to rethink its message and restate it in simple and precise terms.

This requires at least two efforts on the side of the Christian church.

We should take seriously the challenge of Marxism in the field of modern sciences. There can be no doubt that Christianity was not very well prepared to meet the unavoidable shock which the appearance of the "sputnik" caused on the human scene. In its victorious language communist propaganda has claimed ever since that man, by conquering outer space, has finally disposed of any faith in God the creator. In other words, the traditional Christian world-view (*Weltbild*) is totally destroyed. It would not be wise to pass over this charge in silence, nor to defend the Christian faith by traditional arguments only. We cannot describe this task in full just now, but I should like to point to some attempts to tackle it.[13]

A similar task concerns the Christian service in the world of today. Lenin used to ridicule the concept of "suffering" within the Orthodox church. He spoke with open contempt of Christianity which to his mind had neither the intellectual courage nor the personal power to attack the evils of society. "Communism gets things done" — it is this conviction which lends a sense of superiority to many young people within the sphere of Communistic influence. Christianity will have to be aware of the fact that there are large regions of modern life in which *one* Christian language only will be understood — the language of selfless service and sacrifice.

The third element which we discovered in Marxist thinking constitutes the strongest challenge to Christianity. That noncommittal attitude of Western intel-

[13] Cf. Hanns Lilje, *Der Christ im planetarischen Zeitalter* (Hamburg, 1960).

lectualism is far the most dangerous phenomenon of our day. It is not easy to take a definite side in that battle which is raging right now between intellectuals and anti-intellectuals in Western Europe. One weakness, however, cannot be passed over. It is a fact that the intellectual usually shrinks from making decisions. There is a widespread attitude of being satisfied with observations, criticisms, remarks, and there is sometimes so little power of real, genuine change. Our theological concepts of conversion have changed considerably during the last hundred years, but we cannot pass over the fact that there must be some new start, some change, some demand upon men. It is a well-known fact that dictatorial systems sometimes draw the enthusiastic approval of the younger generation for the simple reason that they "get things done." The idea of obedience and dedication sometimes is more clearly developed in totalitarian systems than in the average bourgeois attitude of Christian tradition.

5

ATHEISM IN THE WEST

IT IS fairly obvious that these few remarks do not constitute the full answer to the challenge presented by militant atheism. We cannot escape the question whether Western Europe is at all in a position to meet it sufficiently and adequately.

It is in this context that we have to face another type of atheism, *atheismus subtilis sive philosophicus*. In doing so, we do not turn just to another variation of atheism which we might observe with a detached curiosity, but we are suddenly faced by the very core of Western mentality. We shall not waste any time in refuting the claim of so many Westeners to defend the Christian tradition against communism. This is just not the case. No careful student of the spiritual scene of Europe can overlook the fact that an atmosphere of atheism covers the intellectual and spiritual life of Western Europe as well as that of the East, only in a different form. We have to remember at this point that we do not speak in terms of anti-theism, but of atheism in the proper sense. Modern European thinking does not stand in any need of a theistic concept.

No fierce struggle is going on, no cries of *Ecrasez l'infâme*! God just does not appear in average European thought.

This statement, of course, needs further qualification.

The pith of this attitude of mind is most clearly expressed in Jean-Paul Sartre's statement: "What man needs is to find himself again and to understand that nothing can save him from himself, not even a valid proof of the existence of God."[14] In other words, he is not concerned to disprove God; but he insists that God's existence, even it it could be proved, would make no difference. There is no doubt that Sartre is an atheist, a plainspoken, almost blatant atheist. But his statement goes far beyond traditional atheism. God does not matter any longer. Whether he exists or not, he is completely disregarded. Can there be any more outright attack upon traditional Christianity than this?

The situation appears even more dangerous if we turn to the noble counterpart of Sartre, the Nobel Prize winner Albert Camus, whose tragic and premature death at the beginning of 1960 all of us remember. He was almost a theologian who disbelieved in God; his thirst for divinity was so great that he seemed to resent God for not existing. In his lecture to the Dominicans of Latour-Maubourg in 1948[15] he dissociated himself in no uncertain terms from a nonreligious pharisaism which looks with contempt upon traditional Christianity; but at the same time he made it quite clear that he

[14] Jean-Paul Sartre, "Existentialism," in *Existentialism from Dostoevsky to Sartre,* ed. Walter Kaufmann (New York: Meridian Books, 1956), p. 311.
[15] Albert Camus, *Actuelles I.*

did not share the Christian belief in God. It is not nar-row-minded obstinacy, but a deep sense of tragedy and injustice, which makes him say at the end of his famous letters to a former German friend: "I know that Heaven which looked with indifference upon your terrible victories will look with the same indifference upon your final defeat. Even today I do not expect anything from him."[16] The fact that this indictment does not stem from any vulgar hatred makes this attack upon traditional Christianity even more vigorous.

At this point we should remember the second among the three characteristics which we discovered in the atheistic propaganda of the East — namely, its claim to a strictly scientific basis. Modern scientific thought has had such a deep influence upon the modern mind, has shaped and molded it to such an extent that any metaphysical argument must be looked upon with utter distrust. The "style" of modern thinking does not favor any metaphysical outlook. Speculation and meditation have been replaced by experimentation. It is not surprising that religion is not rated very highly in an intellectual atmosphere which believes in scientific precision and to which religion must appear vague, unrealistic, and outdated. The spiritual climate of this generation does not seem to be favorable to a belief which cannot be put to test in the same way as the scientist controls his world. But this very fact should keep us from passing judgment on this type of atheism. For it compares most favorably with a certain type of thoughtless traditional Christianity. Jacques Maritain,

[16] *Ibid.,* p. 38. The letter is from July, 1944.

the Roman Catholic writer, has an interesting remark in his book *The Range of Reason*[17] in which he comes to an intriguing comparison between the atheist and the saint. The serious atheist has a daring faith, a "greatness and generosity," because he sees through the idols which lure most people into devotion. He risks disapproval. In this sense he is very close to the saint who lives by the "total, stable, supremely active refusal to accept things as they are." Only the saint rejects *all* idols, including the atheistic ones of nature and society. By this radicalism which the atheist shares with the saint, he may be closer to God than those who believe in God, but only in a vague and lukewarm manner. We still believe that the gospel has the answer to the atheist, but certainly not a cheapened and tamed version of the gospel.

We have to pay attention, therefore, to a third type of atheism which is not well defined but very widespread in Western Europe today. We suggest the term *atheismus practicus,* which is borrowed from the great biblical scholar Johann Albrecht Bengel (1687-1752). In his famous New Testament commentary *Gnomon Novi Testamenti* he points out that the rich man in the Lord's parable (Luke 16:19-31) was not condemned for any heresy but because he lived by a certain *atheismus practicus,*[18] disregarding God and eternity. This formula, though it is more than two hundred years old, seems to me an excellent description of the most difficult spiritual phenomenon in the Western world of

[17] New York: Scribners, 1952.
[18] Johann Albrecht Bengel, *Gnomon Novi Testamenti* (editio prima, 1742; 8th ed., Stuttgart: 1891, p. 284).

today. For it suggests exactly what it says: not an explicit anti-theistic theory, but the actual and practiced disregard of God. Here is not apostasy but weakness, not an open revolt but silent paganization. Again the term "paganism" should be taken in its original meaning. The *paganus* of the declining Roman Empire was the person who was driven back to the countryside and into the backwoods, still clinging to the belief in the old Roman deities, but already yielding to the rushing up of new nations and a new faith. The old religion was dwindling, drying up, slowly disappearing, and with it went the intellectual strength of a whole civilization. In a similar way practical atheism is up to this day closely linked to a certain intellectual provincialism, at least as far as "metaphysical" and "religious" categories are concerned. We may put the same observation in a slightly different way: the very specialized knowledge of the scientist is frequently linked up with a strange naïveté in religious matters — at least in the mind of the reading public. New insights of modern physics which might have caused giddiness in Newton are manipulated casually by the average reader, while at the same time some of the simplest expressions of Christian religion seem to be beyond comprehension by him.

Now it would upset all standards of precision if we would take these observations as the basis of a charge which Christianity has to bring against the "modern mind." Here is reciprocity. The metaphysical weakness of modern man is part of the failure of Christianity to find its way between the unchanging and unchangeable substance of God's revelation in Christ on the one hand and the necessary adaptation of our message to modern concepts on the other hand.

But we must not think of this weakness of the West as an intellectual phenomenon only. In addition to this spiritual impoverishment and this intellectual uncertainty there is to be found a weakness in the life of the Christian and the church. Sometimes there is no longer any fierce atheistic attack, because Christianity seems to have had its day. It no longer shapes the life of the individual or influences public life. People sometimes have a hard time in finding out what Christian categories are still valid and effective in the daily life of Christian congregations and individuals. This is noted by Christians as well as by non-Christians. Members of the "younger churches," that is to say, Christians from Asia and Africa, sometimes wonder whether there might be a connection between the lack of simple, straightforward Christian language and the lack of simple obedience in a Christian way of life in European Christendom. The eye of the critic sees even more clearly. C. W. Ceram, author of a book which overtook all other publications in the German language and became a fantastic bestseller, recently published a pamphlet, *Provocative Notes,* in which, among other provocations, he sums up the situation of Christianity in a similar way.[19] The very fact that Christianity lost its public influence, together with its simplicity of speech and life, indicates that the time of "high reli-

[19] C. W. Ceram, *Provokatorische Notizen* (Hamburg, 1961).

gion" has passed, and that of Christianity, too. Love, simplicity of faith and conviction, readiness for sacrifice, including the sacrifice of one's own life — these were the categories by which the early church conquered the world. Are they lost for good?

6

THE CHRISTIAN RESPONSE

THERE is not much to be said in answering these charges. No theoretical program can lead the church back to its source of life. No apologetic discourses will convince the skeptic that the church is still alive. Renewal can only be the result of repentance, renewed faith, and fresh obedience.

At this point we realize anew that the East-West relationship in Europe is not only a geographical or political, but a spiritual problem as well. In conclusion we shall try to sum up the few main lines of Christian reorientation.

The Christian church in Europe is more afflicted by the political division than most people realize. The church in Germany bears the marks of this open wound in its own body. But the division among all the churches on this and the other side of the Iron Curtain plays a big role in their public life.

Two obvious tasks follow out of this state of affairs.

In the first place, the churches have to think of one another in a new understanding of vicarious suffering. We in the West may feel over and over again the helplessness of our longing hearts while we would love to alleviate the burden of our Eastern brethren. All we can do is to remember them in constant intercession and to try to find ways and means to exercise actual fraternal love. And this may lead us to a new appreciation of the meaning of prayer and brotherly assistance. Needless to say, this should not be done in any form of patronizing attitude. We in the West are certainly not the *beati possidentes* who share their goods with the needy brother. On the contrary, there is so much that will come to us as a gift and spiritual blessing. It must have its effect on the church in the West, if the church in the East is put to the test and stands its ground. Christians in the East live under visibly reduced circumstances, and the possibility of expressing their faith is reduced, too. But at the same time they are reduced to fundamentals. There is not that confusing variety of public relations, but one way and one method only. In this situation the Word of God regains its sterling value. This little scene is typical, and has occurred more than once. A debating group is assembled under the leadership of a party functionary. The meeting maintains a stubborn silence. The party man starts chiding the church in order to evoke some sort of discussion. Whereupon one participant, a worker, rises and says simply: "Thus says the Lord: Heaven and earth shall pass away, but my words shall not pass away." We in the West could only with difficulty imagine a similar scene; but it strengthens our faith if we notice this power of the Word of God, when it is reduced to the simplest form of witness.

In the second place, the churches in the West must

use their opportunities to the full. Space forbids a complete description of their tasks, but three avenues of thought and action may be mentioned briefly.

The Christian church in the West has a unique political responsibility. It is not necessary to emphasize that a "crusader's ideology" is not an expression of a specifically Christian attitude. On the contrary. Though it is the Christian's right and duty to take a firm stand in the political controversies of Europe, he will do so in the spirit of his Lord, who did not come to destroy men's lives, but to save them (Luke 9:56). He will maintain that objectivity which could be one of the noblest contributions of the Christian church to the political life of Europe, and which is the best safeguard from prejudice, hatred, and fear, which are so terribly interrelated and from which man cannot liberate himself without divine assistance.

The most important contribution which the church can make, however, is its very existence. A real and living Christian church is bound to be a fact of the highest political importance. For it could be the source of strength and insights which all the people of Europe need so badly. Not by striving for political "power," but by just being the church which tries to listen to its Master.

There is no doubt that in maintaining this attitude the church will also be a guardian of those precious riches of European culture and history which all of us value so highly. If the church resists the temptation to make this its primary goal, then — and only then — it will experience the truth that "all these things shall be added unto you."

For Further Reading

By HANNS LILJE:

Atheism, Humanism, Secularism. Minneapolis: Augsburg, 1964. A further treatment of some of the themes outlined in this booklet.

The Last Book of the Bible. Philadelphia: Muhlenberg, 1957. Indicates the significance of the book of Revelation for a Christian interpretation of history.

The Valley of the Shadow. Philadelphia: Muhlenberg, 1950.

On Europe and on Communism

HERMAN, STEWART W. *Report from Christian Europe.* New York: Friendship, 1953. Still valuable for its description and analysis of the postwar situation in church and society.

FRAKES, MARGARET. *Bridges to Understanding: The Academy Movement in Europe and America.* Philadelphia: Muhlenberg, 1960. Study of an important aspect of the Western churches' response to the new challenges.

JASPERS, KARL. *The European Spirit.* London: SCM, 1948. Brief statement by a famous philosopher of what makes Europe Europe.

KOCH, HANS-GERHARD. *The Abolition of God: Materialistic Atheism and Christian Religion.* Translated by Robert W. Fenn. Philadelphia: Fortress, 1963. Thorough study by an East German pastor now teaching in the West.

ADLER, ELISABETH. ed. *Here for a Reason: Christian Voices in a Communist State.* Translated by Leslie Seiffert. New York: Macmillan, 1964. How it looks to those who have chosen to stay in East Germany.

BENNETT, JOHN C. *Christianity and Communism Today.* New York: Association, 1960; paperback, 1962. Revised edition of a basic work.

TOBIAS, ROBERT. *Communist-Christian Encounter in East Europe.* Indianapolis: Butler University, 1956.

Facet Books Already Published

Social Ethics Series:

1. *Our Calling*
   by Einar Billing (translated by Conrad Bergen-doff). 1965
2. *The World Situation*
   by Paul Tillich. 1965
3. *Politics as a Vocation*
   by Max Weber (translated by H. H. Gerth and C. Wright Mills). 1965
4. *Christianity in a Divided Europe*
   by Hanns Lilje. 1965

Biblical Series:

1. *The Significance of the Bible for the Church*
   by Anders Nygren (translated by Carl Rasmussen). 1963
2. *The Sermon on the Mount*
   by Joachim Jeremias (translated by Norman Perrin). 1963
3. *The Old Testament in the New*
   by C. H. Dodd. 1963
4. *The Literary Impact of the Authorized Version*
   by C. S. Lewis. 1963
5. *The Meaning of Hope*
   by C. F. D. Moule. 1963
6. *Biblical Problems and Biblical Preaching*
   by C. K. Barrett. 1964
7. *The Genesis Accounts of Creation*
   by Claus Westermann (translated by Norman E. Wagner). 1964

8. *The Lord's Prayer*
   by Joachim Jeremias (translated by John Reumann). 1964
9. *Only to the House of Israel? Jesus and the Non-Jews*
   by T. W. Manson. 1964
10. *Jesus and the Wilderness Community at Qumran*
    by Ethelbert Stauffer (translated by Hans Spalteholz). 1964
11. *Corporate Personality in Ancient Israel*
    by H. Wheeler Robinson. 1964
12. *The Sacrifice of Christ*
    by C. F. D. Moule. 1964
13. *The Problem of the Historical Jesus*
    by Joachim Jeremias (translated by Norman Perrin). 1964

Type used in this book
Body, 12 on 14 Garamond
Display, Garamond
Paper: White Ibsen E. F.